SHACKLETON'S EPIC VOYAGE

RAYMOND BRIGGS

Text by Michael Brown

COWARD-McCANN New York

FIRST AMERICAN EDITION
TEXT © 1969 BY SHOWELL STYLES
ILLUSTRATIONS © 1969 BY RAYMOND BRIGGS
LIBRARY OF CONGRESS CATALOG   CARD NUMBER   69-1495
PRINTED IN GREAT BRITAIN

"Stand by to abandon ship!"

The command rang out over the Antarctic seas, and it meant the end of all Ernest Shackleton's plans. He was the leader of an expedition which had set out to cross the unknown continent of Antarctica. It was a journey no one before him had ever attempted.

For months his ship, the *Endurance*, had been trapped in ice. It drifted helplessly in the Weddell Sea, over 400 miles east of the Antarctic mainland and 1,200 miles south of the southern-most tip of South America. The pressure on the hull of the *Endurance* was extreme, and the ship's timbers groaned under the strain.

Now Shackleton's first goal was to lead his men to safety. They would try to cross the polar sea on foot, head for the nearest tiny island, 250 miles to the west.

Slowly the men climbed overboard with the ship's stores.

Shackleton, a gaunt bearded figure, gave the order "Hoist out the boats!" There were three, and they would be needed if the ice thawed.

Two days later, on October 30th, 1915, the *Endurance* broke up and sank beneath the ice. In the bitter cold, the chances of survival seemed small. But spurred on by Shackleton the 27 men set off, dragging their stores and the ship's boats on sledges across the uneven ice.

For five months the crew of the *Endurance* pushed their way slowly northwest across the frozen seas. Sometimes they dragged the sledges painfully behind them. Sometimes they drifted on large ice floes that slowly split into smaller and smaller pieces until they had to be abandoned. At times they took to the boats and sailed or rowed through melting ice. At last, in April 1916,

they reached Elephant Island—a tiny, barren, rocky outcrop 540 miles from the nearest inhabited land, Port Stanley in the Falkland Islands.

By now the situation was grim. Food and other supplies were low. Still worse, five months of constant cold and hardship had weakened all of the men. They were in poor condition to face the coming winter.

Seeing this, Shackleton knew that he and his crew could not last much longer. He decided on a desperate attempt to find help before winter set in. He turned to the men. "We will make our camp here. Six of us will take the *James Caird* and try to reach Stromness. It's our only chance." Stromness was a whaling base on the island of South Georgia, 800 miles N.E. of Elephant Island. To reach it they must cross some of the stormiest seas in the world.

The *James Caird* was the biggest of the ship's boats. Even so she looked pitifully small to face the great grey seas of the southern ocean. Shackleton had the keel strengthened and added make-shift decking to give more shelter.

By April 24th all was ready, and the *James Caird* was launched from the beach. Some of the crew were soaked to the skin as they worked; this could be deadly in the bitter cold and wind so they changed clothes with those who were to stay behind. Shackleton shook hands with the men he was leaving, and then amidst cheers the *James Caird* set sail.

The little knot of men left behind was dwarfed by the high peaks of Elephant Island, and was soon lost from sight.

The *James Caird* was alone on the vast heaving seas. With one arm gripping the mast, Shackleton guided the boat through the ice floes that threatened to hole the sides. At last they were in clear water and, with a fair wind, set their course for South Georgia.

STORES TAKEN IN THE *JAMES CAIRD*

FOOD

30 boxes of matches	3 cases sledging rations
6½ gallons primus fuel	2 cases nut food
1 tin methylated spirit	2 cases biscuits
1 box blue lights	1 case lump sugar
2 primus stoves	30 packets powdered milk
1 Nansen cooker	1 tin beef cubes
6 sleeping bags	1 tin salt
A few spare socks	36 gallons water
Candles and blubber oil	112 lb. ice

Now began a fierce ordeal for the crew of the *James Caird*. The boat was small and crowded. It was almost impossible for the men to find space among the stores and the rocks carried for ballast. All cooking must be done over a single primus stove that needed three men to handle it. One held a lamp, the other two lifted the cooking pot off whenever the violent pitching of the boat threatened to upset it. A fine spray of water constantly soaked its way through the flimsy decking.

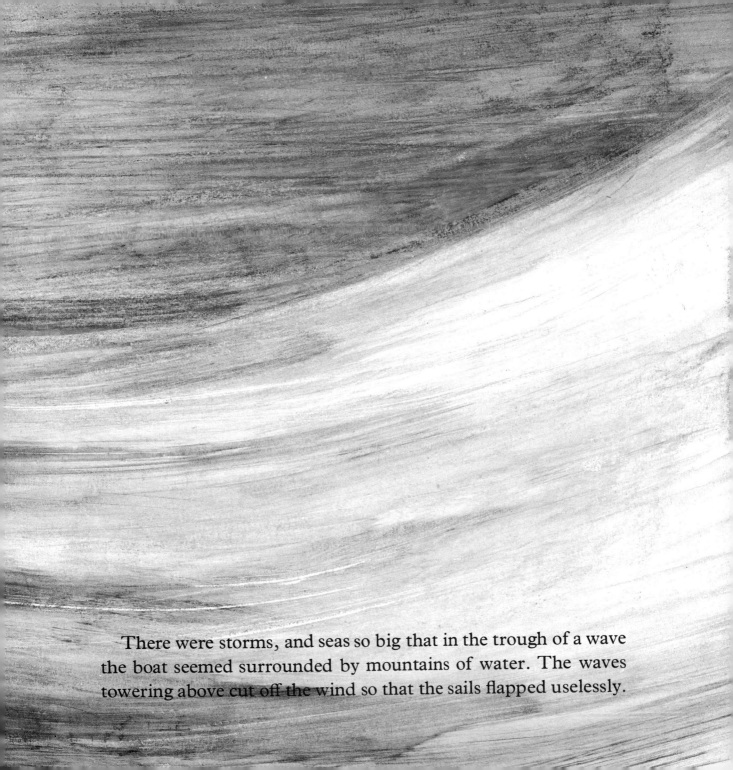

There were storms, and seas so big that in the trough of a wave the boat seemed surrounded by mountains of water. The waves towering above cut off the wind so that the sails flapped uselessly.

Four days passed. A gale sprang up that threatened to swamp the *James Caird* and hurl her crew into the icy seas. "Lower the sails," shouted Shackleton, above the roar of the wind. "We'll heave-to under bare poles and lie to the sea anchor." The sea anchor was a triangular canvas bag at the end of a long line which held the bows of the boat into the wind. If the seas hit them sideways on, they would capsize.

No man aboard had faced such waves before. Sometimes looking out abeam they could see a great tunnel formed as the crest of a towering wave hung toppling over its base, then broke. Time after time it seemed they *must* be overwhelmed, but they survived.

The spray shot at them like burning arrows. It froze thick on the canvas decks and the bare masts, and would soon make the boat top-heavy. Shackleton saw the danger. "We must get the ice off, or we'll capsize," he warned.

Some of the men struggled on to the heaving deck and chipped ice away with axes to free the boat of the deadly weight. Others hurled things overboard—spare oars and sleeping bags—anything they could do without that would lighten the load.

At last on the morning of the seventh day, the wind dropped. The sea calmed, the skies cleared, and for the first time the sun shone. Thankfully, the men dragged out sleeping bags and sodden clothes and hung them in the rigging to dry. Cape pigeons flew overhead and porpoises played in the sea alongside. Shackleton and his men lay on deck soaking up the warmth. Hope surged in them; life was not so miserable after all.

For three days they sailed steadily on, and then a gale hit them like a blast from a great gun. Sun, pigeons and porpoises disappeared. Snow squalls and huge waves hid everything from sight. At midnight Shackleton was at the helm when he thought he saw a break in the sky. Was the weather clearing? Then, to his horror, he realized that he was looking at the foam-capped top of the most gigantic wave he had ever seen!

"For God's sake, hold on! It's got us!" he shouted from the helm. The breaking wave seized the boat and flung it forward, out of control, with the sea surging and foaming around it. Water poured in. "Bail for your lives!" cried Shackleton.

The men bailed frantically. At last they had flung enough water over the side to be safe, but conditions aboard were now much worse. Everything was drenched, there was not a dry place in the boat. For three hours they struggled to light the stove and boil up some milk to warm themselves against the biting cold.

The next day the weather was better, but now there was a new danger. The water supply was running out. Unless the *James Caird* reached South Georgia soon, her crew would die of thirst.

Shackleton and his men were weary and down-hearted. Tortured by thirst, they sailed listlessly on, believing that the end was near, yet hoping to sight land. Then on the morning of the fourteenth day, they saw two shags perched on a mass of seaweed. These birds never flew far from shore. Surely, surely land was near.

At noon, through a break in the clouds, Shackleton glimpsed the dark cliffs of South Georgia. It was a glad moment.

He steered the boat inshore, looking for a landing place, but everywhere rocky reefs or sheer cliffs barred the way. Night was closing in and there was no hope of getting ashore until next morning. It was a bitter disappointment to spend another night at sea.

But that same night another storm blew up. As hours passed it swelled in strength until the wind was hurricane force. Nothing could be seen through the driving spray. The *James Caird*, tough as she was, strained to the utmost so that her seams cracked open and water poured in. To add to this nightmare, the wind swung round and drove the boat slowly backwards, towards the dangerous coast they had seen the day before.

When all seemed lost, a miracle happened. The wind dropped and shifted to blow them offshore. They were saved from the reefs! But not from the torment of thirst. Shackleton knew they must land soon and find water. After one more night at sea, the boat neared the shore again. They could see a wide bay. The wind was rising and Shackleton decided he must run for that bay and take his chance. But as the *James Caird* neared the entrance, the crew saw that the way was blocked once more by a line of rocks like broken teeth. The sea thundered over them sending up fountains of white spume.

The men braced themselves. They were sure that the *James Caird* would be dashed against the rocks.

Suddenly Shackleton shouted to the helmsman. He had seen a narrow gap. The next wave carried them forward and through this opening, so narrow that they could almost touch the rocks on either side. Then, at last, they were safe in calm water. In the gathering darkness they beached the boat and Shackleton leaped ashore. At his feet ran a stream of fresh water and in a minute he and his crew were on their knees slaking their thirst. The worst was over.

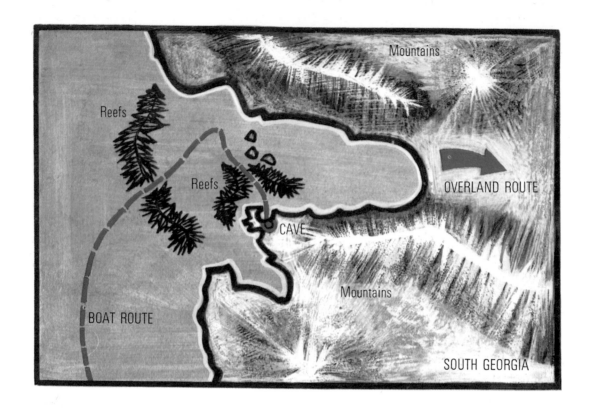

Now Shackleton and his men began to explore the cove where they had landed. They found a small cave in which they lit a fire, and for the first time in two weeks they spent a night ashore. But a long and perilous journey was still ahead.

The whaling station at Stromness lay beyond high mountains which had never yet been scaled. Shackleton set off with the two strongest members of his party, leaving the others with enough food for a few days.

The mountains rose 4,000 feet and the three men were often forced to turn back. They had no tent and kept going through the night, resting now and then, but not for long. They were exhausted but knew that if they stopped they would freeze to death.

Early the next morning they heard a strange sound. It was shrill and high pitched, eerie, spine tingling.

But it did not, after all, signal their death. It was a man-made sound—a steam whistle calling the men of the Stromness whaling station to work.

Shackleton and his men topped a final ridge. Below them were huts and distant figures.

In astonished silence the workers watched as Shackleton and his men staggered towards them, like creatures from some earlier savage time. Two little boys took one look and ran, terrified by the sight of the ravaged, bearded faces and tattered clothes.

But the epic journey was over. Rescue of the entire crew was now certain. By his courage, Captain Shackleton had led his men through the perils of ice, thirst, wind and storm. They had challenged the sea and won.